LONDON TRAVEL GUIDE 2023

THE MOST UP-TO-DATE POCKET GUIDE TO THE CITY OF MUSIC | LONDON'S ANCIENT HISTORY, ART, CULTURE AND HIDDEN GEMS TO PLAN AN UNFORGETTABLE TRIP

BY

MIKE J. DARCEY

© Copyright 2023 - All rights reserved.

It is not legal to reproduce, duplicate, or transmit any part of this document in either electronic means or printed format. Recording of this publication is strictly prohibited and any storage of this document is not allowed unless with written permission from the publisher except for the use of brief quotations in a book review.

Table of Contents

INTRODUCTION 5

CHAPTER 1. THE HISTORICAL OVERVIEW OF LONDON 9

    THE CULTURAL HERITAGE, ART AND ARCHITECTURE 14

CHAPTER 2. LONDON ITINERARIES 16

CHAPTER 3. LONDON'S MAIN ATTRACTIONS 30

    THE HOUSES OF PARLIAMENT 31

    THE LONDON EYE 32

    THE BRITISH MUSEUM 33

    WESTMINSTER ABBEY 34

    CAMDEN MARKET 35

    MADAME TUSSAUDS 36

    HYDE PARK 38

    MORE ATTARCTIONS 39

    THE HIDDEN GEMS OF LONDON 41

CHAPTER 4. THE LOCAL CULTURE 48

    HOW TO AVOID TOURIST TRAPS 53

CHAPTER 5. THE BEST RESTAURANTS, CLUBS AND NIGHTLIFE 59

    THE TYPICAL LONDON FOODS AND DRINKS TO TRY 67

CHAPTER 6. ACCOMMODATIONS 73

    ACTIVITIES TO DO AS A FAMILY 80

CHAPTER 7. TRANSPORT 82

    BUSES 84

    RAILWAYS 85

CHAPTER 8. SEASONS AND WHAT TO PACK 89

The currency exchange 94

Introduction

Whether you're visiting London for the first time or are a seasoned traveler, there's always something new to see and do in this vibrant capital city.

While the main attractions are always a must-visit, you should also explore less-known neighborhoods, local markets and museums for a more authentic experience. This way, you'll discover the true essence of London.

Things to Do

London is a cosmopolitan and buzzing city that boasts plenty of attractions, museums, and activities to keep you busy throughout your trip. While you should definitely see the main attractions that London has to offer, there are a few hidden gems that will make your visit to the city even more memorable.

The British Museum is a bucket list must-see for most visitors to the UK, with tens of thousands of artefacts from around the world. You could easily spend an entire day exploring this opulent collection of antiquities and ancient artifacts, from historic Britain to Japanese and Egyptian art to Benin artefacts from Nigeria.

If you're a Harry Potter fan, don't miss the Warner Brothers Studios. The studios are just outside of London and they're the perfect place to learn more about how the movies are made, while getting a glimpse of some of your favorite characters in their natural habitat!

The West End is home to many of the top musicals and shows in London, including favorites like Mamma Mia and Les Miserables. You should also go to the Royal Albert Hall, which is a beautiful building with tons of history that you should not miss out on!

If you're looking for some green space, Hyde Park is a great place to walk around and enjoy the sunshine!

Where to Stay

If you're planning a trip to London, you'll want to book your accommodation in advance. The city's hotels fill up fast, and prices go up considerably once the traditional work week ends. There are some great options, including the Hilton Canary Wharf and Park Plaza Westminster Bridge.

You'll also want to consider your budget when booking a hotel in London. You should aim to choose somewhere that's in a reasonable price range and isn't far from important sights such as the London Eye or Tower Bridge.

Some of the best places to stay in London include Covent Garden, Mayfair, Kensington and Chelsea, and Notting Hill. These areas are known for their luxury hotels and are a good choice for those who want to be close to the most popular attractions in the city.

Another area that's often overlooked by first-time visitors is London's east end, where you can find some of the city's most exciting nightlife.

Notting Hill is a popular neighborhood with visitors for its antique shops, quaint cafes, and artsy neighborhoods. It's also home to the world-famous Portobello Market, which is famous for its street art and boutique shops.

You should look for accommodation that's close to the metro system in London, which can save you money by cutting down on taxis and other transportation expenses. A good option is The Portobello Hotel, which is less than a mile away from Notting Hill Gate metro station.

For a more quiet and calm experience in the city, consider an apartment instead of a hotel room. These are especially convenient for families or groups traveling together.

There are plenty of things to see and do in London, so you should take your time to explore the city and find your perfect accommodations.

For the best travel experience, consider getting an Oyster card, which is a contactless payment system that can be used on the Underground, buses, and other forms of public transportation. It also helps with planning your journey by allowing you to buy your tickets in advance and avoid the need for paper tickets.

The bike-sharing system in London, run by Santander, has 11,500 bikes dotted around the city with more than 750 docking stations. These are accessible with a credit card at a docking station or from the app, and the first 30 minutes are free.

Biking can be a great way to see the city and is a fun and inexpensive alternative to renting a car, especially for those traveling solo or on a budget. However, it is important to remember that cycling in the busy streets of London can be dangerous and there are traffic signs reminding visitors of this.

The quickest and most convenient way to travel in London is by the famous London Underground subway system, affectionately known as "the Tube". This widespread and efficient system stretches from Heathrow Airport - one of the world's largest airports - into central London.

Most stations have multiple exits, and many attractions are signposted to make sure you don't miss your destination. To get the most out of your journey, download the free app City Mapper and use it to determine how long your travel time will be, based on where you are going and which transport option you want to use.

If you don't have a smart phone, you can always purchase a London Transport map at a tube station. These maps are incredibly useful and will help you find your way around quickly.

It is a good idea to try and travel during off-peak times, which is when the price is usually cheaper. These are generally between 7:30am and 8:30am in the morning, and from 4:30pm to 7:00pm in the evening.

Chapter 1. The historical overview of London

London has a history of over 2000 years that stretches from the Roman Empire through to modern times. The city has grown and prospered while enduring many unfortunate events.

Origins

During the Roman period, it was known as Londinium and was an important port on the River Thames. It was a thriving commercial centre, as well as being a base for Roman military forces in the region.

After the Romans were defeated by the Iceni in 43 AD, London began to flourish as an economic focal point and mercantile hub for traders. The location of the city also made it an ideal place to send supplies from Europe to Roman troops in the area.

The early years of London were difficult, but the city gradually grew in size and importance throughout the medieval period. This growth was partly due to the influx of immigrants from across the continent, which swelled the London population, and increased trade in the surrounding areas.

A major event that shaped the future of London was the Norman Conquest, which led to the establishment of the Tower of London and the formation of London's self-government. This allowed the city to elect a mayor and enforce laws within its limits, allowing it to become an important political centre.

Another major change that took place was the building act of 1666 which decreed that all new houses should be built of brick and to a standard design. This helped to shape the architecture of London for many years to come.

During the Tudor period, there was a great influx of new residents, many from foreign countries, as England sought to expand its empire. This meant that the city became a hotbed of trade, as well as becoming an important cultural and intellectual hub.

Growth

A booming economy and a strong commitment to social policy by the government have allowed London to maintain and grow its population. The latest census showed that Greater London was home to a total of 8.77 million people. The city continues to grow, with an expected increase of a further 8.8 million by 2021.

There are many reasons why the city has a higher than average population, but some of the main ones are economic and cultural. The city is known for its highly skilled labour force, and as a global business centre it offers opportunities for people who can develop their talents.

The rapid growth of the city, however, has not come without consequences. This pressure has pushed up housing prices across the whole of the capital, as well as driving up rents in London's outer suburbs.

This has led to an increase in the number of families in London, which has contributed to the broader demographic shift that we see today. As a result, the city's population has become more dense than ever before. This means that the city's infrastructure is increasingly overburdened, and more people are relying on private transport to get around.

This is not something that should be ignored, and the city needs to find creative solutions to ensure that more family-friendly, climate-friendly housing can be built within its municipal boundaries.

It is important to note that this growth is not taking place in the same way as the previous growth - the city's population has been growing in a more progressive manner, with a larger proportion of people living in inner suburban areas than ever before. While this growth is happening, the City of London has to make sure that it is able to deal with the increased demands on its public services.

Characteristics

London is a city that has a lot of character. It's not only an incredibly cosmopolitan place, but it's also one of the world's oldest cities. The characteristics of a city are important to understand so that you can choose the right location when looking for a new home or an investment property.

1. Physical features of the city

It also has many tributaries and streams that flow into the Thames.

2. The environment of the city

London has a very clean and green environment.

3. The economy of the city

London is an economic hub for the United Kingdom. The city is known for its world-class businesses and many international companies have their headquarters in the area.

4. The transport system of the city

The UK's transport network focuses heavily on London, which makes it easy for people to travel around the country and even internationally. This includes the motorway network, the rail network and multiple airports.

5. The population of the city

It has a population of over a million and it is growing rapidly. This is a result of the fact that the city has been able to attract employment opportunities.

6. The culture of the city

There are a number of things that make the culture of the city so unique. Some of these include the theatre, art, music and food.

The culture of the city is very important and it plays an important role in attracting tourists to the area. The city also has a large number of museums and galleries that offer an excellent experience for visitors to the area.

Endings

The early 20th century saw a period of great change in London. It became a major center for culture, commerce and politics. The city's population grew rapidly and public transport was expanded. In addition, the city developed many new attractions.

As the city's commercial importance grew, it became increasingly important as a centre of government. It began to supplant Winchester as the centre of power in England. In 978 King AEthelred the Unready issued the Laws of London from the city, and in 1016 Edward the Confessor was responsible for founding Westminster Abbey and moving the witan there.

A large part of the population moved to the town in the 14th and 15th centuries, as Britain's trade expanded. In the 15th century London grew as a major European centre for mercantilism, with foreign merchants living in places such as Vintners Place and Dowgate.

In the early 20th century, the city's commercial success encouraged a new wave of immigration. A huge number of people moved to the city from different parts of the world, and this resulted in the population growing considerably.

Another notable development was the emergence of an aristocratic society. During the Tudor period, the Royal Family expanded its power and influence, becoming one of the most powerful monarchs in history.

The Tudor period also saw the beginning of the Peasants' Revolt, when rebels led by Wat Tyler stormed London in 1381. The revolt was short lived, and the city's authorities quickly restored order.

The cultural heritage, art and architecture

The cultural heritage architecture includes buildings and structures of historical or cultural significance that are important to the nation, and require conservation. In the UK, there are almost 400,000 officially recognised heritage assets.

The architectural heritage of a society is influenced by its identity, culture, and social values. Conserving these values makes the architectural heritage valuable and attractive to the community, which is why it must be protected.

Historical significance

London has a vast and complex history that stretches back over two millennia, making it one of the most historically significant cities in the world. Founded by the Romans in AD 43, it quickly became the capital of Roman Britain and developed into a vital center of trade and commerce. Over the centuries, it has been the site of numerous historical events, including the Great Fire of London in 1666, the Blitz during World War II, and the birthplace of the Industrial Revolution. The city is home to numerous historic landmarks, including the Tower of London, St. Paul's Cathedral, Westminster Abbey, and the Houses of Parliament, which are all significant tourist attractions and symbols of London's rich history.

Aesthetics

London's architecture is a blend of historic and modern styles that make the city unique and beautiful. The city's skyline is dominated by iconic structures such as the Shard, the London Eye, and the Gherkin, which are world-renowned architectural marvels. London is also known for its stunning parks and gardens, including Hyde Park, Kensington Gardens, and Regent's Park, which are popular attractions and provide an oasis of calm in the midst of a bustling city.

Social value

London is a diverse and multicultural city that attracts people from all over the world. It is home to over eight million people, speaking over 300 languages. The city is renowned for its world-class education and healthcare systems, providing access to top universities, hospitals, and research institutions. It is also a hub for art, music, and culture, with numerous museums, galleries, and music venues. The city's cultural diversity and vibrancy make it a significant social and cultural center, attracting people from all walks of life.

Economic value

London is one of the world's leading financial centers, with a thriving economy that generates significant revenue and employment opportunities. The city is home to numerous multinational corporations, financial institutions, and startups, making it a hub for innovation and entrepreneurship. London's economy is diverse, with strengths in finance, technology, media, tourism, and creative industries. The city is also a vital transportation hub, with several international airports, rail connections, and a comprehensive public transport system that facilitates trade and commerce.

In conclusion, London's historical significance, aesthetics, social value, and economic worth make it one of the most dynamic and influential cities in the world. It continues to attract people from all over the world, making it a cultural melting pot and a symbol of diversity and innovation.

Chapter 2.
London itineraries

Here are some itineraries to help you make the most of your time in this amazing city:

Classic London Tour:

This tour covers the must-see sights of London, including Buckingham Palace, the Tower of London, Big Ben, the Houses of Parliament, the British Museum, and the National Gallery. This itinerary can be completed in 3-4 days.

Day 1: Buckingham Palace, St. James's Park, Trafalgar Square, and the National Gallery.

Day 2: Tower of London, Tower Bridge, and the Shard.

Day 3: British Museum, Covent Garden, and the West End.

Day 4: Houses of Parliament, Big Ben, Westminster Abbey, and the London Eye.

London Museums and Galleries Tour:

Day 1: British Museum and the British Library.

Day 2: National Gallery and Tate Modern.

Day 3: Victoria and Albert Museum and Science Museum.

Day 4: Museum of London and National Portrait Gallery.

London Parks and Gardens Tour:

This tour takes you through some of London's most beautiful parks and gardens, including Hyde Park, Kew Gardens, Regent's Park, and Hampstead Heath. This itinerary can be completed in 2-3 days.

Day 1: Hyde Park and Kensington Gardens.

Day 2: Kew Gardens and Richmond Park.

Day 3: Regent's Park and Hampstead Heath.

London Markets and Shopping Tour:

This tour is perfect for shoppers and foodies. It takes you through some of London's best markets, including Camden Market, Portobello Road Market, Borough Market, and Brick Lane Market. This itinerary can be completed in 2-3 days.

Day 1: Camden Market and Portobello Road Market.

Day 2: Borough Market and Covent Garden.

Day 3: Brick Lane Market and Oxford Street.

London Nightlife Tour:

This tour is ideal for those who want to experience London's vibrant nightlife. It covers some of the best bars, clubs, and entertainment venues in the city, including

Soho, Shoreditch, and Camden. This itinerary can be completed in 2-3 days.

Day 1: Soho and Covent Garden.

Day 2: Shoreditch and Hoxton.

Day 3: Camden and King's Cross.

No matter which itinerary you choose, London is sure to enchant and captivate you with its endless charms and attractions.

Harry Potter Tour:

This tour is perfect for Harry Potter fans and takes you through some of the locations that inspired and featured in the iconic Harry Potter series, including Platform 9 3/4, the Leadenhall Market, and the Warner Bros Studio Tour. This itinerary can be completed in 2-3 days.

Day 1: Visit Platform 9 3/4 at King's Cross Station, the Leadenhall Market, and the Harry Potter Shop at Platform 9 3/4.

Day 2: Visit the Warner Bros Studio Tour London - The Making of Harry Potter.

Day 3: Take a Harry Potter walking tour of London.

London Architecture Tour:

This tour is ideal for those interested in architecture and design, and takes you through some of London's most iconic buildings and structures, including the Tower Bridge, the Shard, the Houses of Parliament, and the London Eye. This itinerary can be completed in 3-4 days.

Day 1: Visit the Tower Bridge and the Tower of London.

Day 2: Visit the Shard and the Houses of Parliament.

Day 3: Visit St. Paul's Cathedral and the London Eye.

Day 4: Visit the Sky Garden and the Barbican Centre.

London Food Tour:

This tour is perfect for foodies and takes you through some of London's best culinary delights, including traditional British cuisine, street food, and international cuisine. This itinerary can be completed in 2-3 days.

Day 1: Visit Borough Market and try some street food.

Day 2: Take a food walking tour of Soho and Covent Garden.

Day 3: Visit Brick Lane Market and try some international cuisine.

No matter which itinerary you choose, London has something for everyone, and you are sure to have an unforgettable time exploring this amazing city.

7 days London tour

A 7-day London tour will give you plenty of time to explore the city's many attractions, museums, parks, and neighborhoods. Here's a sample itinerary:

Day 1: Arrival and Exploring the City

Arrive in London and check-in to your hotel. Take a stroll around the city center and explore some of the nearby sights, such as Trafalgar Square, the National Gallery, and the British Museum.

Day 2: Classic London Tour

Take a classic London tour, visiting some of the city's most famous attractions, such as Buckingham Palace, the Tower of London, Tower Bridge, and the Houses of

Parliament. End your day with a ride on the London Eye for a stunning view of the city.

Day 3: Museums and Galleries Tour

Day 4: London Neighborhoods Tour

Explore some of London's unique neighborhoods, such as Camden, Shoreditch, and Notting Hill. Take in the street art and eclectic markets of Camden, the trendy bars and restaurants of Shoreditch, and the colorful houses and famous Portobello Road Market in Notting Hill.

Day 5: Day Trip to Windsor Castle and Stonehenge

Take a day trip outside of London to visit two of England's most iconic attractions: Windsor Castle and Stonehenge. Marvel at the grandeur of the castle, and ponder the mysteries of the ancient stone circle.

Day 6: London Parks and Gardens Tour

Spend a day exploring some of London's beautiful parks and gardens, such as Kew Gardens, Regent's Park, and Hampstead Heath.

Day 7: Departure

End your London tour with a food tour, visiting some of London's best food markets, restaurants, and cafes. Depart London in the evening, or extend your stay for more exploration.

This 7-day London tour will give you a taste of everything the city has to offer, from history and culture to food and nature.

GREATER LONDON

Tips on when it is best to go sightseeing, how to get around safely, and mistakes to avoid to save time and money while traveling in London

Whether you're looking to explore the famous sights or simply enjoy a day walking around, there are several different times of the year that will suit your preferences and budget.

If you want to do sightseeing without battling crowded tourist attractions, then visiting during the off-peak seasons is the way to go. During these months, you can expect to find better airfare prices, fewer crowds at attractions, and more affordable hotel rates.

Spring

Spring in London is the ideal time to enjoy the city's dazzling array of attractions. Cherry blossoms bloom in the spring in many of London's parks and green spaces, including Kew Gardens and Holland Park. You can stroll through these beautiful floral-laden spaces and take photos of them for Instagram.

Hampstead Heath is another popular London park, with its sweeping views of the city and huge hilly expanse. It's also a great place for a day out and a picnic with the family.

One of the biggest world-heritage sites in London, Kew Gardens is a must-see for botanical lovers. Visitors can stroll through the gardens and even go inside the glass garden rooms.

The park is also home to the London Zoo, which is always a hit with kids. It's an exciting, educational experience that will keep them occupied for hours.

There are lots of other outdoor activities you can do during the spring, too, including a trip to an indoor theme park and a day spent exploring the many museums that line London's streets. The weather can be a little damp, though, so it's worth taking an umbrella.

It's also the perfect time to watch a show at a London theatre. This includes the classic Medea at @Sohoplace or the delightful Shirley Valentine at the Duke of York's.

For those who like a bit of adventure, the river boat races at the Thames are a great way to spend a sunny spring afternoon. These events are popular among both tourists and locals, so make sure you bag your spot early!

If you're looking for a unique way to spend a spring evening, check out one of the many outdoor cinemas that have recently popped up in London. These are a great way to unwind after a busy day sightseeing and they are a lot more fun than a typical Friday night out at the drive-in!

Summer

The best time to do sightseeing in London and stay safe is when the weather is pleasant. The summer is a popular time to visit London because it usually offers warm temperatures and long daylight hours.

It is also a good time to see the famous sights and landmarks in London such as Buckingham Palace. However, you should remember that the summer is a busy time for tourists and attractions may be less accessible due to high crowds.

If you prefer a quieter and more intimate visit, January or February is a good time to do sightseeing in London.

You should also take advantage of the many festivals and events that happen in the city during this time. Some of the most notable include:

- Bonfire Night - The first week of November is known as "Bonfire Night" in England, and it's a great chance to celebrate this national holiday.
- Christmas - This is a very special time to visit London, as there are many festivities going on during this period. Besides the Christmas lights and decorations, there are also special events like the famous Totally Thames festival.

The autumn is also a good time to visit London, as it offers mild weather, 11deg to 15degC (52 to 59degF) and a wide range of annual events to attend. The October half-term is a great time for families to visit, taking advantage of the school holidays.

Winter is another great time to visit London, as it offers a nice temperature and many events to take part in. The rain can be a bit heavier than during the spring and summer, but it's not as cold as it is in the summer.

Fall

Autumn in London can be beautiful, with crisp temperatures and gorgeous leaves in the city's parks and commons. You can also enjoy a number of events and festivals that take place during this season. Halloween and Guy Fawkes Night are two of the most popular, so you'll want to plan accordingly if you plan to attend any of them.

The weather starts to get a little cooler and rainier around this time, but it's not as humid as in the summer.

Fall is a great time to visit London, and it's a good idea to choose your travel dates carefully to ensure that you can take advantage of the best conditions. The fall season runs from September to November, and there are a number of reasons why you should consider visiting this time of year.

During this season, the city's parks fill up with locals and tourists, beer gardens overflow, and you'll have more time to explore your favorite attractions. However, you'll have to prepare for a few more days with rain and some chilly temperatures, so it's important to pack warm clothes and a waterproof jacket before you go.

Meteorologists divide the year into quarters based on average temperatures and use this as their definition for autumn. This means that it can be quite a bit colder and rainier during this season than during spring or summer, but the days are still relatively long.

It's also a great time to explore some of London's most famous museums, as they host some of their best late night events during this period. In addition to its wonderful weather, the fall season is also a great time to visit London because it is less crowded than during the summer months. Many of the most popular attractions and museums offer special discounts or deals at this time of year, so you'll be able to enjoy your stay in London for a much lower price.

Winter

During the winter, London's attractions tend to be quieter. This makes it a great time to visit museums and galleries, especially if you don't want to be surrounded by crowds.

The crowds can be quite busy at these locations, but they're not as big as those at other popular destinations during the summer or around major holidays.

For more active travelers, consider taking a walk or biking through one of London's parks. These are great places to enjoy the fresh air and work off any extra Christmas calories! The Winter Wonderland market in Hyde Park is one of the most popular events in the city.

You can also head to Borough Market, which is an old-school London attraction that's perfect for a cold day. The market is filled with stalls selling everything from handmade clothes to fresh produce, and it's also where you can buy mulled wine to warm up during your visit.

You can also check out the weather forecast before your trip to London so that you know what kind of weather to expect during your stay.

Mistakes to avoid to save time and money while traveling in London

London is a popular destination for travelers, but it can be confusing. Many first-time visitors make mistakes that end up costing them money or time in London.

1. Not Planning Ahead

It's a good idea to make sure you plan ahead when traveling in London. It's not only helpful to have an itinerary, but it also helps avoid unnecessary costs.

Planning ahead is especially important if you're visiting London during the summer season, when travel is at its hottest and prices are at their highest. As a result, it's a great idea to snag discount passes and advance fast-track tickets for popular attractions in advance, such as the London Pass.

Another great way to cut down on your expenses while traveling in London is to eat at restaurants that offer discounts when booked in advance. These offers are often available online or in local newspapers, but they can also be found on signage outside of some restaurants and bars.

You can also find bargains on a variety of items during certain times of the year, such as during festivals or on "3 for 2" sales at drugstores and bookstores. These sales gimmicks are usually marked by stickers on the front tables or special signs on store shelves, so be sure to look for them!

Finally, if you're staying in London for several days, consider taking at least a few day trips from the city.

Using an Oyster card or Visitor Oyster is the cheapest way to travel in London and can help you save a lot of money. You can also use a contactless payment card to pay for your tickets in London!

2. Not Taking Public Transport

The city offers everything from historical sites to delicious restaurants and gorgeous views. It's also full of cultural diversity, making it a fantastic place to explore.

You can use daily travelcards, ordinary contactless credit cards or "Oystercards" to ride the subway, buses and other public transportation in London. Just be sure to check your ticket before you ride, as some zones and routes will have different fares than others.

When you're planning your trip to London, it's a good idea to download an app that will help you navigate the city. It will show you the best ways to get from point A to point B, as well as giving you specific bus stops.

The app is free to download and it's a great way to plan your trip. Another option is to buy a tourist card, which can save you money on public transportation, and gives you access to a range of free attractions.

Even if you don't end up using public transportation much, it's still a good idea to get an Oyster card before you arrive. It's much cheaper than buying single tickets and it gives you access to all of the regulated public transportation in the city.

If you do end up needing to use public transportation, it's important to avoid overusing it. The Tube is one of the most used modes of public transportation in London, and you can easily waste your time on it if you're not careful.

In addition, it's best to avoid riding the Tube during rush hour. This can be especially frustrating for travelers with bags or those who have limited mobility.

Similarly, it's often better to avoid going to major attractions when they're most crowded. Trying to get to the top of the Tower of London, for example, during the peak of the day will be more stressful than fun and could cause you to miss out on some great experiences.

3. Not Taking A Road Trip From London

There are so many things to do and see in London - it's impossible to cover them all in just a few days. Instead, it's best to spend at least a week or two here to get an understanding of what the city has to offer.

During your time in London, you should also take advantage of the many free attractions.

If you have a family with young children, be sure to check out the many museums that are free for kids! They are often some of the best in the world and a great way to educate and entertain your children while you're in London.

To further save money, consider buying a day pass to the London transport system. This will help you to travel around the city and also make navigating the tube much more efficient.

It's also a good idea to shop around for prices on items like food and toiletries. There are many places to purchase these goods, but some stores, like Tesco and Aldi, can be cheaper than others.

Similarly, if you have any specific requests for your trip, you can always ask the concierge in your hotel to recommend some cheaper options. Just be sure to let them know what you're looking for ahead of time to ensure that they can meet your expectations.

Finally, be sure to avoid peak times in the UK, such as July and August, when the weather is often rainy. These are the times when crowds can be a real issue and prices can spike. This is especially true during Easter and Christmas, when there are more visitors than usual.

4. Not Having Emergency Contacts

London is a huge city and it's easy to get lost and find yourself spending money in places that aren't necessarily necessary. For example, if you're traveling with family or friends, make sure to have their contact information on hand and keep it in your phone so that they can contact you in the event of an emergency. This way, your loved ones can stay in touch and know that you are safe and sound.

If you're planning on visiting some of London's most famous attractions during your stay, it's worth checking out discounts and offers ahead of time. Another good idea is to look for a discount visitor card that lets you save money on entrances to popular attractions, such as the London Pass. This works like a travel card but is much cheaper than buying single tickets with cash (order yours before you go to start saving immediately!).

The same goes for buses and trains. A cheap way to use public transport is to get an Oyster card that allows you to travel on all of Greater London's transport systems for a set price. You can also save money by using a contactless payment card, such as Visa or Mastercard.

Finally, if you're visiting for a few days and don't want to use your phone too much, consider getting a prepaid data card that allows you to avoid any expected roaming charges. These cards are available from most major mobile phone networks in the UK and will provide you with generous data allowances for a small cost.

In addition to all of these tips, it's also vital to remember that safety is always a key priority. It's not uncommon to be confronted with scams and shady characters in London, but you can always use your common sense and be vigilant if something doesn't feel right.

Chapter 3. London's main attractions

London is a city with endless attractions and entertainment. Its historic sites, castles, museums, and countless pubs are just a few of its highlights.

Its famous landmarks – including the iconic 'Big Ben' and Westminster Abbey – are a must-see for anyone visiting the city. However, don't be afraid to explore the city's lesser-known attractions and get a deeper insight into this cosmopolitan capital.

The Houses of Parliament

It is also a favourite venue for political debates and Prime Minister's Question Time, where MPs are able to challenge the government. There are many attractions on site, and the famous clock tower Big Ben is just across the river.

There are tours of the palace available which provide an insight into its history and features. These buildings are very historic and have been used for parliamentary meetings since the 13th century. The White Chamber was built by Simon de Montfort and the Painted Chamber was built by Edward I, though a number of changes were made to both buildings over the years.

The current building was reconstructed after a fire in 1834. It is not without its flaws and many people feel it needs to be replaced. Currently, there are plans to move Parliament out of the palace while building works take place. However, there are backbenchers who oppose this.

The London Eye

The London Eye is one of London's most iconic attractions, and a must-do for any tourist. This giant observation wheel, which sits on the South bank of the River Thames, is 135 meters tall and offers spectacular views of the city skyline.

It was erected in 1999 to celebrate the Millennium celebrations, but its popularity prompted it to be made permanent. Since then, millions of visitors have enjoyed a bird's-eye perspective on the city's landmarks from its vantage point.

Unlike the Ferris wheel found in many panoramas, the London Eye is not meant to be a thrill ride; it circles slowly around, offering unobstructed views of the city. The view is not just limited to the city's top sites, however; you can see all the way down the River Thames to Windsor and even the English Channel.

The London Eye offers a number of different tickets including standard, fast-track and family. The standard ticket is a good option for most visitors, but be aware that there may be queues at some times, especially on weekends and school holidays.

In addition to offering a stunning perspective on London, the London Eye also features a winter ice rink beneath its wheel. This rink is a fun alternative to taking a ride on the wheel itself, and you can buy a combination ticket that allows you to use both the London Eye and the ice rink during your visit.

The British Museum

The British Museum is one of London's most famous attractions, boasting a massive collection of artefacts that span two million years of history. This neoclassical building is the UK's most visited tourist attraction and is a great way to explore Britain's rich culture.

Originally housed in Montagu House, the museum was established by an act of Parliament in 1753 when Sir Hans Sloane bequeathed his vast collection to the nation. The original collection included antiquities, manuscripts, and books, but over time it grew to include a broad range of other objects including natural history specimens.

In 1823, architect Sir Robert Smirke began building a new neo-classical museum to replace Montagu House and he completed the building in 1852. The centrepiece of the new building was the Reading Room, a huge domed chamber that is now encased in a striking glass-roofed Great Court designed by Sir Norman Foster.

While the majority of the museum's collections are displayed in galleries, there are also numerous special exhibits that are available throughout the year. The next to open in 2023 will be "Luxury and Power: Persia to Greece," which delves into the Greco-Persian Wars and examines how power was gained and lost through luxury.

Westminster Abbey

Westminster Abbey has a long history and is one of the most famous religious and historical landmarks in London. It is a UNESCO World Heritage Site and has been the official burial place for 17 monarchs since King Edward the Confessor.

It is also home to a number of famous people such as Sir Isaac Newton, Charles Dickens and Laurence Olivier. It is the place where Prince William and Kate Middleton married in 2011.

Among the highlights of this 900-year-old church are the Coronation Chair, used in coronations since 1308, and Poets' Corner, which houses the tombs of more than 100 writers. Some of the most notable names here are Geoffrey Chaucer, Edmund Spenser, Samuel Johnson, Robert Browning, Lord Bryon, Alfred Tennyson and CS Lewis.

Camden Market

Camden Market is a hive of activity, combining shopping with regular entertainment events and festivals to attract Londoners and visitors. With a mix of stalls selling everything from designer clothes and hand-made crafts to street food stalls, it's one of the city's most vibrant markets.

It's also home to FEST Camden, a club and art space that draws Londoners and visitors looking for cutting-edge music and dance performances. It's part of an area that was once industrial, but which has since become a center for alternative culture and artists.

The market has a wide range of fashion options for women and men, from trendy clothing stores to vintage-style boutiques. You can also find a number of hip children's clothes.

You can also find shops dedicated to Goth and Steampunk styles as well as outdoor stalls selling bags, shoes, and assorted goods. There's even a record shop that sells actual vinyl!

Madame Tussauds

The museum was founded by Marie Tussaud, a French sculptor who learned the craft from her mother's employer. She made her first sculpture at the age of 16 - a figure of the famous French Enlightenment writer, Voltaire.

It's a fascinating place to go, but be sure to book your tickets in advance. This way, you'll avoid the queues and get a great price for your Madame Tussauds entry.

In addition to a variety of life-like wax figures, you'll find fun interactive zones and a Marvel Super Heroes 4D movie experience. You can also buy a "See London Your

Way" ticket which allows you to combine your visit with other popular London attractions such as the London Eye, the London Dungeon and Big Bus tour.

The process of creating a wax statue takes six months, with 300 photographs and precise measurements taken into account. It is then sculpted from 2,400 pounds of wax. Then it's groomed with hair washes and makeup touches. Some celebrities have to model multiple times before their figure is perfected.

Temple Church

Temple Church is one of London's oldest places of worship and it's also one of the most fascinating - you can really sense how old this place is and it has a beautiful design. As you enter, the circular structure of the church reminds you of the Holy Sepulchre in Jerusalem.

Originally built for the Knights Templar, the church has a round nave which is supported by black Purbeck marble columns. These columns were the first free-standing columns to be made out of Purbeck marble in England, and they are a key part of the church's architecture.

The church also hosts many concerts and other events, including choir recitals, organ music and lunchtime talks. Its all-male choir, consisting of 18 boys from the City of London School, has a well-respected reputation and performs regularly.

The church also holds a variety of Templar-themed events and exhibitions, so you'll be able to learn more about the history of the Knights Templar. You can also tour Middle Temple Hall, which was home to the Knights Templar until the late 1200s.

Hyde park

Hyde Park is one of the most popular attractions in London, England. It is a huge public park, covering 350 acres of land, located in the heart of the city. Here are some key things to know about Hyde Park:

- History: Hyde Park has a rich history dating back to the 16th century when it was first created as a hunting ground for King Henry VIII. Over the centuries, the park has been used for a variety of purposes, including dueling, public executions, and military drills. Today, it is a peaceful oasis in the middle of a bustling city.
- Attractions: There are many things to see and do in Hyde Park. One of the most popular attractions is the Serpentine Lake, which offers boating and swimming opportunities. The park is also home to a number of statues and memorials, including the Diana Memorial Fountain and the Speakers' Corner.
- Events: Hyde Park is a popular venue for concerts and other events. Many famous musicians have performed here, including the Rolling Stones, Pink Floyd, and Bruce Springsteen. In addition to music, the park hosts

a variety of other events throughout the year, such as the Winter Wonderland festival and the London Marathon.
- Accessibility: Hyde Park is easily accessible by public transportation, with several tube stations located nearby. It is also possible to walk or cycle to the park from many parts of central London. Once inside the park, there are a variety of paths and trails that make it easy to explore.

Overall, Hyde Park is a must-see attraction for anyone visiting London. Its beautiful scenery, rich history, and diverse range of activities make it a great place to spend a day or more.

More attarctions

London is a city that offers a plethora of attractions to visitors. Here are some of the most popular attractions in London:

- Trafalgar Square: Located in the heart of London, Trafalgar Square is a public space that is home to the iconic Nelson's Column and the National Gallery. The square is a popular spot for tourists and locals alike and is often used for cultural events and celebrations.
- Big Ben and the Palace of Westminster: The Palace of Westminster is a historic building that is home to the UK's Houses of Parliament. The iconic clock tower known as Big Ben is also located on the palace grounds. Visitors can take a guided tour of the palace to learn more about its history and architecture.
- The Tower of London: One of the city's most famous landmarks, the Tower of London is a historic castle that dates back to the 11th century. The tower has been used as a royal palace, a

prison, and a place of execution. Visitors can take a guided tour of the tower to learn more about its history and see the Crown Jewels.
- Buckingham Palace: The official residence of the UK's monarch, Buckingham Palace is a grand building located in central London. Visitors can watch the Changing of the Guard ceremony outside the palace gates or take a tour of the palace's state rooms during the summer months.
- Tate Modern: A museum of modern and contemporary art, Tate Modern is located in the Bankside area of London. The museum is housed in a former power station and features works by artists such as Picasso, Warhol, and Hockney.
- Piccadilly Circus: A bustling public square in the heart of London's West End, Piccadilly Circus is known for its neon signs and advertisements. The square is surrounded by shops, theaters, and restaurants and is a popular spot for tourists.
- Tower Bridge: A symbol of London, Tower Bridge is a suspension bridge that spans the River Thames. Visitors can take a tour of the bridge's engine rooms and walk across the high-level walkways for views of the city.

Overall, London offers a diverse range of attractions that cater to all interests and tastes. Visitors can explore the city's rich history, enjoy its cultural offerings, or simply soak up the atmosphere in its lively public spaces.

The hidden gems of London

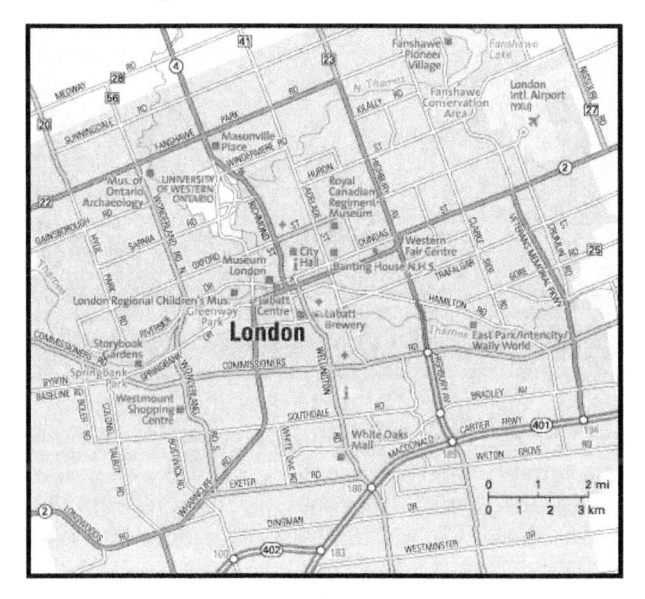

London is a city full of amazing places to see and delicious foods to eat but there are plenty of lesser known spots that can really add an extra thrill to your trip.

From secret gardens and historic pubs to quirky museums and unique shops, these are the best hidden gems in London that you must explore when you're visiting.

Columbia Road Flower Market

Every Sunday, the unassuming road that is Columbia Road bursts into bloom with bucketfuls of gorgeous flowers and plants. It's one of London's best-loved markets and a must-visit on any flower lover's bucket list.

It's a real treat to take a stroll down this narrow street, surrounded by colourful blooms and all the lovely traders who love to chat about the different kinds of flowers they sell.

As well as the flowers, there are lots of interesting little shops, cafes and bars that will make for a fun afternoon of exploration. Whether you're looking for vintage pieces, English and Italian delis or even some quirky vintage clothing stores, Columbia Road is full of the finest independent shops.

The market itself is open from 8am to 3pm on a Sunday. Traders will often offer discounts for early shoppers, so get there before the crowds arrive and stock up on the freshest blooms at this beautiful market in London.

If you're not a big fan of flowers, don't worry: the market is also home to a handful of antique stores, a garden shop, and lots of charming pubs. It's a great place to visit for a leisurely stroll, especially if you're staying in East London, but if you're a bit pressed for time, you can also combine your trip to the market with a quick walk over to Spitalfields Market.

Another great spot to stop for a coffee is the Cake Hole at Vintage Heaven, a charming vintage shop and café that specialises in home-baked cakes and other treats.

Temple of Mithras

In the heart of London, underneath a modern office block, lies one of the UK's most significant archaeological sites. The Temple of Mithras is the remains of a Roman temple which dates back to the 3rd century AD.

It was a home for an all-male cult, which spread throughout the Roman Empire. Its rites were incredibly secret, with no written accounts of the rituals. This cult was known as Mithraism and was believed to have heavily influenced Christianity.

The site was discovered in 1954 by W.F Grimes and Audrey Williams who thought it might be a Christian church, but quickly realised that it was a temple to the god of war, Mithras. The site was soon filled with thousands of visitors, each rushing to see this hidden treasure.

What happened next was a disaster. The reconstructed temple was not a good quality reconstruction, and was built in the wrong place. Then, in 2010, financial information company Bloomberg bought the land and decided it was time to put the temple back where it belongs, so it was reconstructed on its original site.

Luckily, the excavation records produced by Grimes and Williams are so detailed that they can be used as a guide for rebuilding the temple, and the advice of Dr John Shepherd was invaluable to ensure it was done right. The original 1962 version was reconstructed with the wrong stone, and the new one, which stands slightly west of the original site, is more authentic to what we know about the Roman temple.

When you first walk into the space, you're led through an atmosphere of awe and mystery. There's a light show in the main room, and then you're taken down to the basement level where there's an audio loop explaining the history of the temple.

Sir John Soane's Museum

A house museum of a kind that has become as popular as the Wallace Collection, Sir John Soane's Museum is a must for architecture-enthusiasts and art lovers alike. Located next to Lincoln's Inn Fields, it is free to enter and has become one of the most visited places in London.

A neoclassical architect, Soane was responsible for designing several important Regency-era buildings in London including the Bank of England and the Dulwich Picture Gallery. His work drew on classical ideas picked up on an 18th-century grand tour of Italy.

After becoming professor of architecture at the Royal Academy, Soane decided to create a museum within his own home (made up of three buildings in Lincoln's Inn Fields), for his students. The result was a quirky collection of architectural models, copies of famous statues, and artifacts from ancient Egypt, Greece, and Rome.

Visitors are able to view these collections in the museum's many rooms which are packed with furniture, paintings and sculpture. But the best way to experience the museum is by taking a guided tour with a knowledgeable guide who will show you the hidden secrets of the house and explain several fascinating facts about its history.

The collection is arranged in the museum's labyrinthine passages and rooms, which Soane designed himself. The ceilings are studded with skylights, domes and vaults, with sunlight pouring through the stained glass set in them.

Soane had an unusually capricious taste when it came to collecting objects, which is why this museum is so enchanting. You'll find everything from the sarcophagus of Pharoah Seti I to architectural drawings by Piranesi and J. M. W. Turner, as well as some of his own original furniture. In fact, Soane was so enamoured with his collection that he had an Act of Parliament passed to ensure that it would be preserved and kept in the same condition as he left it, a move which ensures that it's as it appears today, untouched since his death.

St Dunstan in the East

Located just minutes away from the Tower of London and the City, St Dunstan in the East is a secret oasis that even locals don't know about. When you find it, it feels like you've stumbled upon something truly magical.

This grade I-listed church was originally built around 1100 and suffered from damage during the Great Fire of London in 1666. After the fire, the church was patched together and a steeple was added to it by architect Sir Christopher Wren.

However, it wasn't long before bombing raids hit London and the church was severely damaged again. The church was finally rebuilt, but only the Wren-designed tower and steeple remain today.

The rest of the ruins were left to nature and have since become one of London's most achingly pretty public gardens. Trees grow through the windows and ivy climbs the walls, creating a lush, green paradise in the middle of the ruins.

As a result, St Dunstan in the East is now one of London's most popular Instagram spots. The garden looks especially beautiful during spring and summer but can also be a little eerie in autumn or winter.

You can visit St Dunstan in the East any time of year, but it's best to go during the weekends when it gets a bit quieter and more atmospheric. This can be a great way to escape the hustle and bustle of the busy city.

St Dunstan in the East is a great place to spend some time relaxing and taking in the sights of the City, and is also close to many other London attractions. It's located between Lower Thames Street and Great Tower Street, with Monument and Tower Hill underground stations just a few minutes away. The ruins of St Dunstan in the East are open to visitors from 8am to dusk, with entry free. The garden is ideal for a day out with the family, or for a quiet stroll on your own. A fountain sits in the centre of the former nave, and the ruins are perfect for taking photographs or enjoying a picnic.

Chapter 4.
The local culture

London, a world-famous capital, is also one of the most culturally diverse cities in the world. Its museums, theatres, festivals, shops and parks offer a wide range of art, music and culture.

London has been home to some of the world's biggest rock acts, such as David Bowie, Led Zeppelin and Fleetwood Mac. It's also a hub for culture tourism, which brings over PS3.2 billion into the local economy and supports around 80,000 jobs each year.

Culture Mile

In the ancient heart of London, Culture Mile is a place where people connect and collaborate. It is home to five leading arts and culture institutions that are internationally renowned: the Barbican, Guildhall School of Music & Drama, Museum of London, London

Symphony Orchestra and the City of London Corporation.

The five partners will come together to transform the area, with imaginative collaborations, outdoor programming and events seven days a week. Major enhancements to the streets and wider public realm will enliven Culture Mile, as it develops into a world-renowned destination.

With a diverse community of city workers, residents, students and cultural and creative industry workers, the Culture Mile is one of the City's most exciting areas. Its blend of ancient and modern is a distinctive feature, with Roman walls, mediaeval churches and livery halls surrounded by new Crossrail stations, modern apartment blocks and a steady pipeline of cutting-edge office developments.

A new Business Improvement District (BID) is establishing in the area securing investment plans totalling more than PS9m over the next five years. The BID aims to promote the culture of the area, making it a family-friendly and worker-friendly place.

Through the creation of a network of partners, Culture Mile will be able to reach and connect with a broad spectrum of businesses across the City and beyond. It will also connect and collaborate with neighbouring boroughs on economic regeneration, education and skills.

To launch the initiative, a Brutalist-inspired identity was developed for Culture Mile that animates the public spaces between the partner organisations. It graphically represents the programme of pop-up performances, art installations and inclusive events that will take place in these spaces over the next decade.

Bloomsbury

Bloomsbury is a microcosm of museums, trees, cafes and the historic home of artists and academics. The district's leafy Russell and Bedford squares are lined with elegant Georgian townhouses, while the British Museum – a world-renowned collection of antiquities – is in the middle of it all.

The district is also home to Alain De Botton's School of Life(Opens in new window) and an extensive play-park, so there's something for everyone to enjoy. It's the perfect place to spend a day exploring the city while being surrounded by some of the best culture in London.

A cluster of academic institutions and bookshops make up this cosmopolitan area, with a lively buzz of students, tourists and locals mingling in the streets. A plethora of cultural and social events take place, from literary evenings to art exhibitions.

In addition to this, there are many theatres in and around the district, making it a great spot for catching some live entertainment. UCL's Bloomsbury Theatre is a great choice for those wanting to see the cream of theatre, while The Shaw Theatre and Regent's Park Open Air Theatre are also good options.

There are many other attractions in the Bloomsbury district, such as the British Library, which has a surprisingly vast collection of books and documents from across the world. It is also home to the Charles Dickens Museum, which displays a large selection of his work.

If you're looking for a good boozy fix, then there are several bars to choose from in the area. These include The Lamb(Opens in new window), which is a beautifully restored Grade II-listed pub that's full of character and oozes charm. Or for a more modern twist, head to The

Coral Room(Opens in new window), which is located inside the Lutyens-designed Bloomsbury Hotel and serves up cocktails with a strong English feel.

Covent Garden

The area of Covent Garden has a long history as a shopping, theatre and entertainment district. It has become a must-see for visitors to London and has been transformed from its fruit and vegetable market days into a thriving, vibrant, culturally rich destination.

It is home to the Royal Opera House, London Transport Museum, 17th-century St Paul's Church and a variety of street performers. A number of high-end restaurants also draw crowds to the area.

Another great place to visit in Covent Garden is the Seven Dials area, a small quaint roundabout located at the heart of the district. This is a classy part of the district where you can find some of the best restaurants and bars in London, including a truly old school French restaurant, a Filipino canteen, a Swedish bakery, and a sustainable members club.

If you're a lover of food, you should definitely stop by Warehouse, a sustainable members' club that opened in November 2021. It has an 80-seater restaurant that focuses on sustainable produce and head chef Brendan Eades works closely with carefully chosen suppliers who share his vision.

In addition to eating and drinking, Covent Garden is also known for its street performers, and you can watch them performing their magic on the streets around the area. This is a tradition that goes back many centuries, and was first recorded in 17th-century diaries.

There is a lot to do and see in Covent Garden, but it can be overwhelming if you don't know where to start. If you're looking to have a memorable experience in this iconic part of London, it's important to have the right tools to navigate the area and make the most of your time in the city.

West End

London's West End is one of the world's most famous and vibrant areas, packed with theatres, shopping and cocktail haunts. It's not just a cultural hub, though - it's also one of the world's largest business districts, comparable to Midtown Manhattan in New York or Causeway Bay in Hong Kong or Shibuya in Tokyo.

It's a district that's been around for centuries, and it's home to some of the best-known theatrical productions in the world. But it's not just shows that have played a big part in this area's history - it's also been the site of some of the most memorable and influential moments in British history.

During the 17th and 18th century, the West End served as a space where high culture was offered to the rich and the elite. The Royal Academy of Arts, for example, offered exhibitions in Pall Mall, while the Pantheon on Oxford Street hosted concerts, masques and balls.

Yet as the 19th century began, the hegemony of the monarchy declined and the aristocracy was replaced by a more diverse class of people. It was in the West End that this new social order was established, and as it grew, a new and more eclectic culture took hold.

This was reflected in the area's music halls and dancehouses. By the 1850s, this had morphed into an atmosphere that drew in the poorer end of society.

The hegemony of the monarchy declined, but the West End still remained an important place for high culture to be enjoyed. It also became a hotbed for the lower-class, whose hedonism persisted in Covent Garden and its surrounding streets.

The last few years have seen a revival of interest in the theatres, and the area's cultural institutions have reemerged as key attractions for tourists. It's a sign that London is back on the cultural map, and that there is a renewed vigour in the creative industries - both of which are important to regaining the city's place as one of the leading tourist destinations in the world.

How to Avoid Tourist Traps

Whether you're a first-time visitor or a seasoned traveller, it's important to be aware of the tourist scams that are prevalent in London. Fortunately, there are several ways to avoid them.

Pickpocketing is a common problem in tourist-heavy areas, so be sure to keep your belongings close at all times. Also, be mindful of your surroundings and be careful when using public transportation.

Do Your Research

There are many things to see and do in London, but it's important to keep your wallet safe and avoid tourist scams while you're in the city. Here are some tips to help you keep your trip safe and hassle-free:

One of the most common tourist scams in London involves booking hotels online that don't exist. This can lead to serious problems and can cost tourists a lot of money.

Another common tourist scam involves people posing as police officers who ask for money or identification. These crooks can steal your money or valuables, so it's important to be aware of this type of scam and stay away from them.

When visiting London, be sure to research the area you'll be staying in and familiarize yourself with the most popular scams in that neighborhood. Also, be careful when using public transportation and avoid walking alone in the dark.

Pickpocketing is a common problem in tourist-heavy areas, so be sure to keep your belongings close and be aware of your surroundings. This includes keeping your wallet in a front pocket and using only trusted Wi-Fi networks.

Likewise, be careful when shopping in London's popular shopping districts, like Oxford Street or Camden Market. Some criminals will even target tourists who are riding the bus or Tube, so be sure to keep your belongings near you at all times.

Fake hotel scams are becoming more common in London, so be sure to do your research before booking a hotel room online. This type of scam can cause you to lose a lot of money, so it's important to be careful when booking accommodations online.

The fake police scam is another common tourist scam in London, so be aware of this when you're traveling in the city. This scam occurs when someone posing as a police officer approaches you and claims that there is a problem with your wallet or passport. The crooks can switch your identification or steal your money.

It's also important to remember that tourist attractions are often overpriced, so be sure to do your research before buying tickets. Some attractions have special discounted days and other discounts, so be sure to check out what's on offer before booking. You can also purchase a London pass that lets you skip the lines at some of London's most popular attractions.

Ask a Local

When it comes to visiting a new country, it can be difficult to know what is worth your time and money. Unfortunately, many tourist attractions are known as tourist traps, and they can leave you feeling ripped off.

One of the best ways to avoid tourist traps while traveling is to ask a local to show you around. A local can help you see London from a new angle, and they may also be able to recommend some great places for you to eat or shop.

In some countries, there are countless local restaurants that offer great food at low prices. But these establishments are often located in tourist-filled areas, so they attract a lot of people from all over the world.

If you're looking to get a good deal on your trip, it is important to find a place that caters to the locals and not tourists. This way, you can enjoy some amazing food and shopping without having to pay exorbitant prices.

Another thing to consider is to look at reviews before you go. If you read a bunch of negative comments about an attraction, it's probably not worth going to. It might just be a tourist trap and you should avoid it altogether.

Tourist traps are usually places that are overpriced or don't have what you are looking for. They can also be places where you will be ripped off by touts or street sellers.

There are a lot of tourist traps in Europe, but you can avoid them by doing your research. You should do a quick Google search for any tourist attractions you plan on visiting, and you should also read reviews online to see what other people have to say about the attraction.

For example, if you're planning on visiting the Eiffel Tower or the London Eye, it is best to do your research first to ensure that these are the right attractions for you. If you haven't done your research, you will most likely end up paying a fortune for something that is not worth it.

Don't Be Afraid to Go Off the Beaten Path

London is a big city that offers a wide range of activities and attractions. However, there are some things you should avoid if you want to have a truly memorable experience during your time in the city.

One of the best ways to avoid tourist traps is to go off the beaten path. This can be done in a variety of ways, such as eating at a restaurant that locals recommend and taking a stroll through quieter streets.

Another way to avoid tourist traps is to not pay the full price for your tickets at attractions. This can save you a significant amount of money on your trip to London.

While this is not always possible, you should avoid places where the ticket prices are too high. If you are planning to visit any of the famous landmarks in London, be sure to research the ticket prices before your trip.

You should also avoid any place that has a long queue or a gift shop. These can be a big turn off for many tourists.

If you're traveling in the UK, don't be afraid to ask for help. There are plenty of people who are willing to give you advice and recommendations on how to get the most out of your trip to London.

The most important thing is to not be afraid to go off the beaten path, as this will allow you to see the true beauty of the city. This will also help you to feel more connected with the local community, making your experience in London that much more authentic and enjoyable.

In addition, you should not be afraid to eat at restaurants that have a reputation for serving quality food. This can be a great way to discover new tastes while you're in London.

You can also try to eat at restaurants that are more affordable than other eateries. This will allow you to save money on your trip to London and enjoy a more authentic experience.

You should also avoid visiting tourist attractions that are popular on Instagram or have a hashtag that attracts a lot of visitors. This can be a huge turn off for many travelers and can lead to a lot of wasted time.

Don't Be Afraid to Ride Public Transportation

London is one of the world's most walkable cities, with plenty of public transit options to get you around without needing to rent a car. The best part is that it's also very cheap to ride. In fact, you can even take a bus for free with a valid ticket.

It's no secret that the Tube is the best way to get around Central London, but it doesn't have to be your only option. There are many buses to choose from in the city, with services running continuously throughout the day and night.

There are also ferry boats that travel along the Thames, such as the Thames Clippers. These are a great option for getting across the river and visiting some of the more popular attractions.

Another great way to see the city is on a double-decker bus! These buses are not the fastest, but they're an excellent way to get a taste of the local lifestyle.

The buses also run through the night, so you can explore after dark if you'd like. Just remember that buses aren't always the cheapest way to get around the city, so you may want to consider hiring a cab or using Uber or other ride share apps.

If you're looking for a more relaxed way to experience the city, try taking a bicycle. You'll find many bike lanes around the city, which have been designed to improve safety for cyclists.

This type of transportation is also very affordable, and it's perfect for families with young children. You can rent a bike from Santander Cycles, for just $2.50 for 24 hours, and they're easy to get around the city.

Lastly, be sure to check out the London Underground map before you arrive. While it might seem daunting, it's actually quite simple to navigate and doesn't take long to learn.

If you're planning on spending a lot of time in the city, consider buying an Oyster Card. You can buy them online, in person, or at the airport. It's also worth considering buying a contactless card, such as Apple Pay or Google Pay. You can use your card to pay for all of your transport and avoid the initial fee on the paper ticket.

Chapter 5.
The best restaurants, clubs and nightlife

London is home to a diverse range of bars, restaurants and clubs that cater for all tastes. Whether you're looking for something a little more upscale, or want to dance until the sun comes up, London has it all.

Inca – an underground restaurant with a Latin American twist – is a must for any dinner and show lover. With ever-changing performances based on the immense cultural diversity of South America, it's the perfect place for a special night out.

Inca

Taking inspiration from the ancient andean culture, Inca takes you on an immersive journey of food and entertainment. Located in the heart of London on Argyll Street, this restaurant combines the latest and greatest Latin American cuisine with live performances from some of the world's most talented performers.

Whether you're looking for a date night out, an evening with friends or an unforgettable experience with the whole family, Inca is the place to go. They offer a range of delicious dishes and drinks that are sure to make your night one you'll never forget.

It's easy to fall in love with this exciting new Latin-inspired venue on Argyll Street, with eye-popping decor that captures the dualities of light and day, dark and moon, as well as stunning Brazilian tiles that twinkle in the light. Step inside down a winding staircase and you'll be instantly transported into a new world, complete with entertainment that celebrates the vibrancy of South America.

They also have a late-night lounge where their lively entertainment continues, and you're sure to feel like a part of the show. You can dance, sing and enjoy a fantastic party atmosphere until the early hours.

The restaurant is the perfect place to celebrate your birthday or a special occasion, so make sure you book a table for the best experience! With the menu offering a selection of dishes from Peru, Argentina and Brazil plus unique twists on classic Latin cuisine, you're guaranteed to have an amazing meal here.

Flippers Roller Boogie Palace

Whether you're looking to party till the wee hours or let loose to the latest underground house and techno, London has plenty of clubs to keep you entertained. With big-name DJs, great LGBTQ+ spaces and some of the world's best clubs dotted around town, there's something for everyone here.

One of the hottest spots in town is Circus, a restaurant and circus themed nightclub that hosts an array of amazing acts and performers. From acrobats, contortionists and fire breathers to hand balancers and hula hoopers, there's an incredible show for every night of the week.

Another must-visit spot is Flippers Roller Boogie Palace. The rink revives Ian "Flipper" Ross' Los Angeles-based roller rink and legendary cultural hotspot, which was known for its Studio 54 on wheels vibes. For three years, it was a mecca of uninhibited fun where a generation of eccentrics and outsiders could boogie to their hearts content.

The new Flippers, launched in West London last year in partnership with Liberty Ross and Kevin Wall, is everything you want from a Roller Boogie Palace – and more. The 34,000 sq ft space houses a roller rink, live music venue, luxe diner and pro skate shop, plus a whole host of other cool things to do.

During opening weekend, the roller rink is teaming up with Brain Dead, a Los Angeles-based collective of creative artists and designers from around the world. They will offer limited-edition products, bespoke DJ sets, surprise appearances and more.

Cache

Cache is a French-Moroccan restaurant located in the heart of London's trendy Shoreditch neighborhood. It is known for its unique fusion of French and Moroccan cuisines and its vibrant atmosphere.

The restaurant offers a diverse menu with a wide range of dishes that are influenced by both French and Moroccan culinary traditions. Some of the most popular dishes at Cache include the lamb tagine, harissa chicken, and couscous dishes. The restaurant also offers a selection of vegetarian and vegan options.

In terms of its ambiance, Cache has a stylish and contemporary interior that reflects its Moroccan and French influences. The restaurant features bold colors and intricate patterns, which create an exotic and vibrant atmosphere. The lighting is also soft and dim, which makes for a cozy and intimate dining experience.

Cache is a popular restaurant in London that is well-known for its delicious food, unique fusion of French and Moroccan cuisines, and stylish ambiance. It is a great option for anyone looking to try something new and exciting in terms of food and atmosphere.

Baba Yaga's Hut

A visit to Baba Yaga's Hut is one of those experiences that everyone should try at least once in their lives. Not only does it have the most amazing cocktails but it also has a killer food menu so you won't feel hungry at all!

In the folklore and legend of Russian shamans, a powerful witch called Baba Yaga lives in a hut that can move around on chicken legs. In some versions, she can grant your wishes (though this may be a stretch).

Another version of Baba Yaga's hut is that it moves between planes of existence, and each time it travels it changes its appearance to the world it's visiting. It can appear circular, hexagonal, and any other shape it desires.

The hut itself is about 15 feet in diameter and sits on two giant stilts that are actually bird-like legs. They can carry the hut over any terrain and can deliver mighty blows to intruders!

As a result, the hut's interior is filled with magic items and fountains of water. Its walls are the equivalent of 5-foot-thick stone.

In addition to her magical properties, Baba Yaga's hut can also grant wishes. If you ask her for something, she will usually either grant it or eat you. She's a powerful witch who can be dangerous to the unwary.

Chiltern Firehouse

The hottest restaurant in London at the moment, Chiltern Firehouse has quickly become a celebrity favourite. Kate Moss, Rita Ora and Suki Waterhouse are just some of the A-listers that have made the pilgrimage to the chic new venue, opened by hotel magnate Andre Balazs who brought The Standard, Chateau Marmont and Mercer hotels on to the London dining scene.

Located inside one of London's first purpose-built fire stations, the building is a carefully restored property from 1889. It was once home to the fire brigade but now has a boutique hotel and bar, serving a curated menu of fine dining dishes from renowned chefs.

What's more, the restaurant is known for its trendy vibe and excellent people-watching opportunities. It's also a popular spot for special occasions, dinner dates, and romantic meals.

A new addition to the Balazs portfolio, the Chiltern Firehouse is a refurbished Victorian fire station that was transformed into a luxury hotel and restaurant by Andre Balazs. The venue is a chic and modern take on classical elegance and has an outdoor terrace that's perfect for soaking up the sun during the day.

The restaurant is a hot spot for nightlife, especially during the week when it transforms into a club night. However, it's not easy to get a table here and there are always long queues. Luckily, there are plenty of other places to try in the area.

Fabric

Fabric is a London institution, known worldwide for its heaving dancefloors and booming beats. The club has been in business since before the turn of the millennium and has played a key role in the underground scene's push into becoming an integral part of the UK's nightlife.

One of Britain's top clubs, Fabric showcases a range of music genres -- techno, electro and bass to name but a few. Its three rooms feature independent sound systems and two of them have stages for live acts. Room One has a vibrating "bodysonic" dancefloor with 400 bass transducers that allow clubbers to experience the low-frequency frequencies of the music being played.

A 2,500-capacity club with three distinct rooms, Fabric is known for its consistently high quality music programming and the hip crowds that flock to the club on weekends. The club is also home to Fabric Records and FABRICLIVE, a monthly CD series that features DJs from the UK's electronic music underground.

Fabric's closure has sparked debate and criticism in the UK, with social media users campaigning to save the club. The club's licence was revoked by Islington Council in 2016 following the drug-related deaths of two teenagers at the venue. However, a coalition of supporters and the mayor of London Sadiq Khan announced that the club will reopen with new operating procedures in place. The club's operators have also committed to a zero-tolerance policy on drugs.

The Typical London Foods and Drinks to Try

If you are planning on visiting London, there are many typical foods and drinks that you should try. From fish and chips to a full English breakfast, here are some of the most popular dishes that Londoners love.

You will also find many types of coffee and tea. Whether you want to drink it in the morning or with dinner, you can find some of the best coffee shops and cafes in London.

Fish and Chips

Whether you're looking for a quick snack or a more substantial meal, London has an excellent food scene. The city is renowned for its delicious cuisine and has been dubbed one of the world's top food cities by both New York Magazine and The Daily Meal.

Fish and chips are a staple of British cuisine, and it's impossible to go to London without trying at least one.

You can find them at a range of street-food stalls, but for a true, authentic experience, visit a local fish and chips shop, locally known as a "chippy."

The fish in traditional fish and chips is cod, haddock or whiting; the batter is made with flour and water, often beer. The fish is fried, and the chips are smothered with salt and vinegar, which gives the dish a softness that Brits love!

Some people also like to add a side of mushy peas, which are a delicacy similar to pickled eggs. These are usually sold as a paid add-on, and they're very popular in Britain.

Another London classic is the Scotch egg. This spherical delicacy is a favorite snack in many countries, but its origins are unknown. It may have originated as a way to keep travelers from running out of money while they traveled.

Despite its poor reputation in the 20th century, London's food has undergone a revolution that has surpassed any stereotype of bad British cooking. The best part is that there are now thousands of restaurants and markets throughout the city that serve delicious, healthy, and affordable meals.

Aside from the classic fish and chips, London is also home to a number of other traditional foods that are worth a try on your next trip. These include the famous Sunday roast, which is a hearty and sumptuous meal that's usually served at pubs on Sundays. You'll also want to try some of the most popular London drinks, like a gin and tonic or a martini.

Full English Breakfast

The full English breakfast is one of the most well known London foods, and a must-try on your trip to London. It dates back to the 1300s and is the traditional start to the day for many people in England and Wales.

A full English is made up of sausages, bacon rashers, fried eggs, mushrooms, black pudding and a few other toppings that vary from region to region. In addition to the standard breakfast ingredients, it typically includes bread and a variety of condiments like ketchup and mustard.

It is also served with a variety of side dishes like grilled tomatoes and baked beans, which are popular in Britain and Ireland. You can also try a pie and mash, which is a dish of meat and mashed potatoes topped with liquor.

Another unique London food that you should try while on your trip to London is cockles. Cockles are a type of shellfish that is seasoned with malt vinegar and white pepper. They are a popular street food in the East End and are a must-try for those who love seafood.

Scotch eggs are another traditional snack that you should try while in London. These spherical snacks are a delicious treat that is enjoyed everywhere from street food stalls to gas stations and often have a high price tag.

Afternoon tea is another classic British tradition that you should try while on your trip to England. It is a lovely way to treat yourself or to spend time with your loved ones while in London. Afternoon tea is usually served with a selection of finger sandwiches, scones with clotted cream and jam, small cakes, and tea.

Pie and Mash

A staple of London's East End, pie and mash is a dish that dates back to the 19th century. It consists of minced beef filling baked in a pastry crust and served with mashed potato, which is scraped over the top. The mash is often served in large quantities and should be smooth and creamy with no lumps of potato.

The mash is often topped with a thin green parsley sauce called liquor that contains no alcohol. It's a dish that is unique to pie and mash shops and is usually made on the premises daily by the staff.

There are many pie and mash shops across London but we recommend going to M Manze on Tower Bridge Road. This shop has been in the family since 1891 and their traditional recipes have been passed down from generation to generation. They have also won many awards over the years and have become a very popular pie and mash destination for tourists and locals alike.

Another great place to get pie and mash is Maureen's Cockney Food Bar in Chrisp Street Market. This is a redoubtable pie and mash shop that has been in business for over 60 years and serves some of the best pies in London.

Eels are another London speciality that can be found at a number of pie and mash shops. These were once a staple in the local area and were caught in the River Thames. Today these eels are usually sold as jellied or stewed eels.

This is a classic British dish that is still incredibly popular around the world. It is a meal that is very simple to prepare and can be eaten by everyone, even those who are not fond of meat can enjoy it.

Bubble and Squeak

When visiting London, you will want to try some of the typical foods and drinks that are part of the capital's culture. These can include dishes that have been around for centuries, as well as newer trends that have come about over the years.

If you're looking for something hearty and filling to eat on your trip, you can't go wrong with bubble and squeak. This dish is popular in the UK and is made with day-old mashed potatoes and a variety of vegetables that are fried to crispness. It's a great way to use up leftovers and can be served with a fried egg on top!

It's also popular for use as a Christmas dish. You can find bubble and squeak made with cabbage in many British Christmas dinners, and it's also a popular choice to use up the leftover veggies after a traditional Sunday Roast.

Another dish that you might want to try while you're in London is laverbread, which is a Welsh dish that consists of boiled seaweed (laver). This unusual savory food can be found grilled on toast and is sometimes served with shellfish.

In the past, this dish was served as a breakfast staple along with bacon, sausages and a fried egg. Today, it's a popular lunchtime snack in pubs and can be found ready to eat at delicatessen counters across the country.

It's a great dish to make with leftovers, so plan ahead and prepare this meal at least a few hours in advance. This will ensure that it will reheat well and taste just as fresh as it did the first time you served it!

Bangers and Mash

Sausage and mashed potatoes, better known as bangers and mash, is a quintessential British dish that combines two staples of the nation's food culture. It's served all over Great Britain in pubs and a recent survey ranks it as the country's most popular comfort food.

Bangers and mash are often paired with onion gravy, which is easy to make at home with just four ingredients (onion, garlic, beef broth/stock, and flour)! This simple meal is also very budget friendly and perfect for a quick weeknight dinner.

The sausages that are traditionally served with bangers and mash are called bangers because of the sound they make when they cook. The term was first used during World War I when meat shortages led to sausages being augmented with fillers, including water and rusk (dry crunchy bread reduced to crumbs).

These fillers expand when cooked, causing them to break open. The sausages in bangers and mash are typically Cumberland pork sausages, but you can use any type of sausage you prefer.

While bangers and mash is one of the easiest recipes to make, it does require some time and attention. A good sausage is important, as well as a quality mash.

You can bake your sausages in the oven or pan-fry them. The method you choose depends on your cooking experience and preference. According to culinary food scientist Lauren Grant, baking bangers and mash is a good option for newer chefs who don't have experience with fried dishes, as it allows them to control the amount of charred surface they create and reduces the chance of bunging.

In terms of gravy, Grant says that the classic bangers and mash sauce is made with onions, garlic, and beef broth/stock, but you can add a bit of red wine vinegar to make it tangier and more flavorful. Alternatively, you can substitute crispy fried onions for the onions in your sauce to give it a different texture.

Chapter 6. Accommodations

London is a sprawling metropolis, where some of the world's greatest historic monuments and palaces sit amidst soccer stadiums, hip art galleries, free museums, street markets and concert venues.

The city is a patchwork of distinct neighborhoods, each with its own flavor and appeal. Where you stay in London will depend on your budget and interests.

Covent Garden

As the name suggests, Covent Garden is one of the best places to stay in London for those looking for a fun and vibrant experience. It's a place where you can see street performers, visit the Royal Opera House, browse the shops and enjoy a wide variety of restaurants.

It's also a great choice for travelers who want to be close to popular attractions in London such as Buckingham Palace, Tower of London and more. The accommodation options here are also varied with a lot of boutique hotels and luxury hotels available to choose from.

There are a number of hotels located in Covent Garden, but some of the most well-known ones include The Savoy and the Ritz. They are the most famous in the city and provide a luxurious, yet comfortable setting for visitors.

If you're looking for a more affordable option, the Mercer Street Hotel is a good choice. It's a modern boutique hotel in Covent Garden that offers stylish rooms with next-generation technology. The staff is friendly and helpful, and the restaurant is a real hit with locals.

The NoMad Hotel in Covent Garden is another fantastic choice, especially for those looking for a luxury hotel. The hotel is a grade-II heritage building that has been completely renovated by interior designers Roman and Williams. Its interiors feature a lot of quirky design elements and art works, as well as hardwood floors and an art deco bathroom.

Its 105 rooms and suites are also fully equipped with Nespresso machines, Hypnos mattresses and free Wi-Fi. The hotel's location is a little closer to Covent Garden than other hotels in the area, so it's ideal for those who would like to be near the main attractions in the city.

A short walk from the renowned Apple Market, the hotel is located near the many attractions that make up this popular shopping and entertainment hub in London's West End. Its elegant car-free Piazza is home to fashion stores, craft stalls and upscale restaurants.

The Royal Opera House is an iconic part of the Covent Garden culture and it's a must-see for anyone who is visiting the area. It's a world-class performance venue and is easily accessible from the area. Its buildings date back to 1858, and you'll be amazed by the amount of talent that is showcased here.

The West End

The West End is a vibrant cultural hub that's home to spectacular shopping streets, a world-famous theatre district and a top-notch restaurant scene.

Whether you're a seasoned London traveler or planning your first trip to the capital, The West End is the place to go for entertainment and culture. The area is dotted with museums, galleries and attractions to suit all tastes and ages.

The West End is also known for its top-notch restaurants and nightlife, ensuring it's one of the most popular destinations in London. Make sure to check out the best places to stay in The West End while you're there so you can experience it all in comfort and style.

Some of the best hotels in The West End are located within the areas of Covent Garden, Soho and Fitzrovia. These areas are well-known for their shopping, dining and nightlife scenes and are surrounded by some of the city's most iconic landmarks.

There are also plenty of other hotels in The West End that cater to a wide variety of needs and preferences. This includes hotels that offer amenities like free Wi-fi, pet-friendly rooms, and fitness centers.

You can find luxury hotels in The West End, such as The Waldorf Hilton Hotel London or AMBA Hotel Charing Cross. You can also find great value in The Cavendish Hotel or The Trafalgar Hotel.

If you're looking for a family-friendly hotel in The West End, you can book rooms in Hotel Indigo at 1 Leicester Square or The Trafalgar, St James, Curio Collection by Hilton. These hotels are close to the many family-friendly restaurants and shops in The West End.

If you're going to be staying in The West End for a longer period of time, it's a good idea to book your room well ahead of time. This way, you can ensure that you get the room of your dreams. There are also plenty of discount hotels in The West End that you can use to save money on your stay.

The City

The City is a buzzy and vibrant area with a good amount of culture to boot. It's a great place to be if you're looking to see the best of London on a budget and is home to many of its top attractions.

One of the best parts about staying in The City is that it's centrally located and easy to reach by public transport. Plus, the neighbourhood is known for its plethora of restaurants and bars. It also features a variety of museums and cultural institutions, including the British Museum and the Science Museum.

In terms of accommodation, The City offers an array of student housing options for students of all budgets. From high-end luxury apartments to affordable studios, there's something for everyone.

When it comes to choosing the best student accommodation in The City, you'll want to take into account your lifestyle, study habits and budget. This will help you narrow down your choices and find a student apartment that's just right for you.

The right student apartment in The City will make your time away from home easier, more fun and less stressful. You'll be able to enjoy all the amenities you need while being close to your school and the rest of London, so you can save on both rent and travel expenses.

Lastly, it's a given that you should book your student accommodation in The City well ahead of your arrival date. That way, you can take your pick from a plethora of en suite student rooms, modern student flats and even traditional student halls.

The City's most impressive feat is its location in the centre of all that is great about the capital, making it an ideal choice for students with a busy schedule. However, it's still important to remember that London is a sprawling metropolis, so you'll want to consider whether your accommodation is in the heart of the city or somewhere closer to the university campus.

Westminster

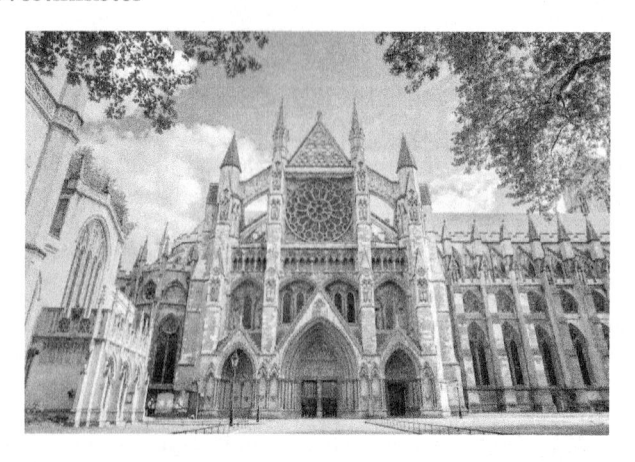

Located on the northern front range of Colorado, Westminster is a vibrant town full of modern shopping and dining, open space parks, and beautiful landscapes. The town is also home to a variety of top hotels, making it an ideal spot for those looking to explore the city and enjoy all it has to offer.

There are a wide variety of accommodations to choose from in Westminster, including traditional hotel rooms and suites. Whether you're traveling alone or with family, there's a hotel for every taste and budget.

The best hotel for you depends on how long you're staying and what activities you'll be doing while in town. For example, if you're planning to spend your time exploring the city, it's recommended that you book a hotel that's close to all of the major attractions.

If you're going to be in town for a longer period of time, it might be worth booking a hotel that offers extended stays and condo-style suites. These types of suites usually feature a kitchen and full bathrooms. Some even have two bedrooms, so they can accommodate families.

Another good choice is SpringHill Suites by Marriott Denver North/Westminster, which offers a mix of modern and rustic decor. This hotel is perfect for business travelers, as they have fully-equipped offices and meeting spaces. For relaxation, guests can enjoy their complimentary breakfast buffet, which includes everything from eggs to yogurt concoctions.

When it comes to finding a cheap hotel in Westminster, look for deals during the low season. Prices drop during the winter months, which are typically February and January.

Alternatively, if you're visiting in the summer, it's probably best to book a hotel that has a pool or hot tub to relax by. The hotels in Westminster that offer these amenities usually have great outdoor views, as well.

The best way to find the perfect hotel in Westminster is to use KAYAK's hotel search tool. The tool will allow you to compare a variety of different hotel options, and will help you find the best price for your stay. It also allows you to search for hotels based on a variety of different criteria, including location, ratings and reviews, and cost.

Activities to do as a family

A trip to London can be a wonderful experience for families, with plenty of opportunities for fun, learning, and bonding. Here are some activities that families can enjoy together in London:

- Visit the iconic landmarks: London is home to some of the most famous landmarks in the world, such as the Tower Bridge, the London Eye, Buckingham Palace, and the Big Ben. A visit to these landmarks is a must-do activity for families in London.
- Explore the museums: London has some of the best museums in the world, such as the British Museum, the National Gallery, and the Science Museum. Many of these museums offer free admission, making them an affordable option for families.
- Take a walk in the parks: London is known for its beautiful parks, such as Hyde Park, Regents Park, and St. James's Park. These parks are perfect for a family walk, picnic, or even a game of Frisbee.
- Enjoy a show: London's West End is home to some of the best theatre shows in the world. Families can enjoy a musical or play together, making for a memorable evening.
- Take a river cruise: A river cruise along the Thames is a great way to see the city and learn about its history. Many river cruises offer commentary and refreshments on board.
- Visit the markets: London has a variety of markets, such as the Borough Market and Camden Market, that offer a range of food, clothing, and souvenirs. Browsing the markets

together can be a fun and unique experience for families.
- Go on a Harry Potter tour: Harry Potter fans will enjoy a tour of the city's Harry Potter filming locations, such as Platform 9 3/4 at King's Cross Station and the Warner Bros. Studio Tour London.
- Take a day trip: London is well-connected to many nearby destinations, such as Windsor Castle, Stonehenge, and Oxford. Families can take a day trip to explore these places and make the most of their time in England.

Overall, London offers a wide range of activities that are perfect for families, from exploring landmarks to enjoying a show. By planning ahead and choosing activities that everyone can enjoy, families can make the most of their time in London and create lasting memories.

Chapter 7. Transport

London is a large city with an extensive public transport network. From the world-famous underground railway system to the famed red double-decker buses, there are many options for getting around London without needing a car.

Taxis are another option, although they can be quite expensive compared to other methods of transportation. There are also many ride share apps that operate in London, like Uber.

Taxis

Black cabs are one of the most popular modes of transport in London. They're known for their safety and reliability. It's also a great way to get around the city, as they can take you anywhere in town.

Taxis in London are regulated and monitored by Transport for London, who make sure that you always get the best service at the best price. They're also responsible for ensuring that all drivers are properly licensed.

To earn their taxi license, drivers must undergo a rigorous testing process. They're required to memorise a labyrinth of streets, avenues and mews that are within a 6 mile radius of Trafalgar Square and a list of 50,000 points of interest in London.

They're trained to drive safely and follow the law, which includes a strict code of conduct. They can't use their vehicle to sell alcohol, and they can't be involved in drug dealing.

You can hail a cab using the yellow TAXI sign on their window, or simply stand on the street with your arm raised. The driver should stop if they see your arm.

In London, black cabs are metered, so you'll pay for your ride at the end of the journey. You can pay cash or by credit card. You can also pre-book your ride in advance through a TfL-licensed private hire operator called a minicab.

When booking in advance, you'll need to provide your booking number and a contact phone number. Usually, a cab driver will call you to confirm the booking.

The price you pay is calculated by the driver's meter, which will be displayed on the dashboard of the car. Depending on the route and your destination, you'll pay a fixed fare or a distance-based fare.

If you're planning to hire a black cab, it's a good idea to book at least 24 hours in advance, especially during peak times. It's also a good idea to pre-book your journey if you're taking a group or planning a large trip, as you'll avoid paying more for each individual member of the party.

There are a number of other types of vehicles available in London, including chauffeur and executive cars, limousines and minicabs. They're not all regulated by TfL, but they can offer cheaper fares than black cabs.

Buses

There are a few different ways you can get around in London. One is through buses and cabs, which are a great way to see the city at a lower cost than the Tube.

London buses are operated by an organisation called Transport for London (TfL). They provide information about routes and timetables, as well as selling tickets for bus, train and tram services. They also publish maps in leaflet form, on their website and as apps for phones.

You can buy an Oyster card, which is a smartcard that you can use to pay for trips on London buses and the London Underground. You can also buy a Day Bus Pass, which is a single-use Oyster card that you can take on any London bus.

Some buses also offer a "hail and ride" service, where you can hail the driver and then let them know where you want to get off. This is particularly useful on outer-London routes that may not have a set stop.

Another option is to get a black cab, which are very reliable and can be booked in advance on your smartphone. They're a bit more expensive than the buses but also have the advantage of being able to take you to where you want to go. A black cab can also be an ideal way to see the city's landmarks, as drivers are well-versed in the area and can point out historical places you might not otherwise be able to find.

When you're ready to leave the bus, just press a red button that is usually found on upright metal posts throughout the bus. This will alert the driver that you want to get off and they can then let you off at a safe place along the route.

In many parts of central London, you can board buses without having to purchase a ticket. This is a good option for tourists who don't want to have to wait in line or pay a higher fare.

Some buses, especially double-decker ones, can be very crowded. To avoid this, try to choose a seat on the upper level of the bus, as this will ensure you have space to move. If you're travelling with a child or a wheelchair, you can often stand on the lower level of the bus as well, though make sure to keep yourself within reach of a pole or overhead handle so that you don't fall over.

Railways

Railways are a major form of transport in London. They are a key component of the city's infrastructure and provide services to over 600,000 passengers per hour in peak hours.

As a city of the world's largest population, it is essential that there is a reliable and efficient way to move people around. One of the most popular ways of doing this is through the underground railway network.

There are four lines on the London Tube: Bakerloo Line, Piccadilly Line, Victoria Line and District Line. These lines run through the heart of London, with each providing a different service to different areas.

The most important line for commuters is the Bakerloo Line, which carries many people in and out of London. The line has received a major upgrade, including new inter-car gangways to increase safety and accelerate trains.

Other main lines are the Northern Line, the Thameslink line and the Overground. The Overground is the only orbital rail network in the country and operates through a concession to Transport for London (TfL).

Although the majority of train journeys are made on the Underground, there are also many long-distance rail services that pass through London. This provides a significant source of income for TfL, which is responsible for all London's public transport infrastructure and railways.

As the number of people who need to commute to work increases, so does the need for more railway stations throughout the capital. This requires investment in new stations and new train technology.

There are many reasons why this is necessary, but one important factor is the rising cost of property in London. This has led to the development of "dormitory towns" outside of the city, where people can live cheaply and still be within easy reach of London by train.

Another reason is the growth of employment in south London and the Docklands. This has resulted in a significant increase in the amount of passengers who use trams to get into and out of the city.

As the number of passengers on London's trams rises, so do the need for more train stations. This is why TfL are planning to extend the East London Line both north and south to cater for the increasing demand.

London's subway system, known as the Tube, is an efficient and affordable way to get around the city. Here are some of the stops on the various subway lines and the main attractions that can be visited from those stops:

Piccadilly Line: This line connects Heathrow Airport with central London and runs through some of the city's most popular areas. Some of the stops and attractions include:

- Covent Garden: Home to a popular market, street performers, and various shops and restaurants.
- Leicester Square: A popular area for entertainment, with many cinemas and theaters.
- Piccadilly Circus: A famous landmark with its bright neon signs and statue of Eros.
- Hyde Park Corner: Provides easy access to Hyde Park, one of London's largest and most famous parks.

Central Line: This line runs through the heart of London and stops at some of the city's most iconic attractions. Some of the stops and attractions include:

- St. Paul's Cathedral: Get off at St. Paul's station to visit the iconic cathedral and climb up to the dome for stunning views of the city.
- Tottenham Court Road: This station is close to the British Museum, one of the most important museums in the world.
- Oxford Circus: This station is at the heart of London's shopping district, with popular stores such as Topshop, H&M, and Selfridges.
- Marble Arch: This station provides easy access to Hyde Park and Speaker's Corner.

Jubilee Line: This line runs from north to south through central London and stops at several famous landmarks. Some of the stops and attractions include:

- Westminster: Get off at this station to visit the Houses of Parliament, Big Ben, and Westminster Abbey.
- London Bridge: This station is close to the Tower Bridge and the Tower of London.
- Canary Wharf: This station is located in London's financial district and has many skyscrapers and restaurants.
- North Greenwich: Get off at this station to visit the O2 Arena, which hosts concerts, events, and exhibitions.

Northern Line: This line runs from north to south through central London and stops at several popular attractions. Some of the stops and attractions include:

- Camden Town: This station is close to Camden Market, one of the city's most popular markets.
- Waterloo: This station is close to the London Eye and the South Bank, which has many restaurants, theaters, and galleries.
- London Bridge: This station is close to the Tower Bridge and the Tower of London.
- Leicester Square: A popular area for entertainment, with many cinemas and theaters.

These are just a few examples of the many stops and attractions that can be visited using London's subway system. With 11 lines and over 250 stations, there are plenty of places to explore and discover.

Chapter 8. Seasons and what to pack

When packing for a trip, it's important to plan clothing based on the season. This will help you pack efficiently so you're not stuck with extra clothes or a suitcase full of unwanted items.

London's weather can be unpredictable so layers are key for your wardrobe. Bringing lightweight warm layers will keep you cozy from day to night while also looking stylish.

Spring

Spring is a great time to visit London. The weather is usually warm, but can occasionally be chilly, so you will want to pack layers. A cardigan can be your best friend during this season, as it can help to keep you cozy and warm - just remember to bring a pair of tights or leggings under it!

Long sleeve shirts are another must have for this season. They are easy to layer under a sweater or cardigan, and they can even be worn on their own in warmer weather.

Dresses are also a must have in this season if you want to take advantage of the sunny weather. You can wear them to restaurants or pubs to enjoy a cool breeze, or even just around the parks.

Denim is another essential for this season. You can choose from classic straight-leg, skinny, or bootcut styles to match your mood and style. If you're traveling with someone, try a matching set of jeans and a dress for an outfit that is both comfortable and stylish.

Shoes are another must have for this season. You'll be walking a lot in this city so you will need to find some that are both comfortable and stylish. Waterproof sneakers, ballet flats or chic boots are a good option for this season, and you can always throw on a pair of socks for extra comfort!

If you're going to be visiting the museums or other attractions, you will probably need to wear a coat. You may want to go for a waterproof jacket or trench coat depending on the forecast, but a light insulated jacket will be a great option on most days.

During spring, it can rain a lot in London, so be sure to pack a raincoat. A small one will fit in your bag and won't be too much of a hassle to carry around.

You can also opt to pack a nice umbrella, but be careful not to bring too large of a one as it will mark you out as a tourist! A small and lightweight umbrella is always a good choice in London.

Summer

When packing for the summer in London, remember that you can still wear short sleeve tops and t-shirts, but you may want to pack a light jacket or cardigan if it gets cooler. You can also try to break out some fun and bright colours to make your outfit pop!

One of the most important pieces to pack in the summer is a pair of light, comfortable shoes. Flat sandals or even a pair of strappy trainers are great options for London in the summer.

Another must-pack item is a comfy, lightweight backpack. This will allow you to bring all of your essentials and not have to lug around a large suitcase.

A backpack will also keep you organized and prevent you from losing items while exploring. You can add any small items you might need for the day, such as a water bottle or wallet, and a couple of books to read while on your adventure.

Lastly, a good pair of sunglasses is also a must-have for the summer in London. A bright and colourful pair will not only look great on you, but they'll also protect you from the sun's harmful rays!

It's also a good idea to add a few scarves to your London summer packing list. They're great as a fashionable accessory to a dress or top, and they're also a great way to keep your hands warm.

The best part is that you can take them on a trip with you and not worry about them breaking, as they are super lightweight and easy to carry around.

When it comes to winter in London, we know that it can be cold and rainy, so we recommend bringing a winter coat to cover your body. You can also pack a hat and gloves for extra protection from the elements.

The Met Office records an average of 106.5 days of rainfall in the UK, so it's inevitable that you'll get some rain during your trip to London. It's not usually torrential, but it can still rain and you don't want to be caught out without a waterproof coat or umbrella!

Fall

The autumn season is a great time to visit Europe, as it's still chilly during the day but the evenings can be crisp and dry. Like spring, the weather is subject to change, so it's a good idea to pack smart.

First and foremost, you'll want to bring something warm enough to wear on your feet during the day. While flip-flops and open-toed shoes are not a good idea, you can dress up sandals with a lightweight cover-up or wear socks to keep your feet from freezing.

For fall's cooler temperatures, a long-sleeved cotton or synthetic-blend button-down with sleeves that can be folded or rolled to the elbow is a smart move. And if you're traveling to a place that sees a lot of rain, you might want to invest in a waterproof coat.

A light cardigan is the perfect backup for an early evening or a night out on the town. If you're a traveler with a tight budget, you can opt for a cheaper option, such as this fuzzy wool cardigan by Calvin Klein.

To ensure your luggage has room for all your cool clothes, consider purchasing a set of quality storage bins that have a special gasket that keeps out air and other dusty contaminants. The right containers will also help you easily find what you need when you need it.

Winter

London's winter season is truly magical, from its enchanting Christmas markets to beautiful lights adorning the city. But if you're visiting London in winter, it's important to remember that the city can get quite cold and wet, so make sure you pack the right clothes for your trip!

A wool coat is a must, as well as warm shoes and socks. You can also invest in a winter hat or scarf, which will be incredibly useful and add some style to your outfit.

If you're travelling to London during the winter, you can look forward to a great range of tours and activities. Some are only available at this time of year, but many others are open all through the winter months.

Take a trip to the Borough Market during your stay in London to sample a variety of traditional British snacks, including mulled wine, hot chocolate and mince pies! This bustling market is always a fun place to visit but it's especially charming in the winter.

Another popular activity during the winter is ice-skating, and there are plenty of rinks to choose from in the city. Taking part in these events can be a lot of fun, and it's a perfect way to keep warm as you see the city from a new perspective.

The best part about ice skating is that you can do it in some of the most beautiful and historical places in London, so this is definitely an experience you should not miss!

When you're in London in the winter, it's easy to forget that you can still enjoy outdoor activities, such as walking in one of the city's beautiful parks. A walk through

Richmond Park or Hyde Park is a great way to soak up the fresh air and watch the deer nibble on the grass.

It can be a bit difficult to know what to wear in the rain, so it's worth packing waterproof shoes and jackets for your London winter vacation. This is especially important if you are planning to travel by public transport.

The best thing about traveling in London during the winter is that it's still possible to visit all the amazing museums and attractions that London has to offer. This includes some of the world's most famous museums, so don't be afraid to explore!

The currency exchange

Currency exchange in London is a common practice due to the city's status as a global financial hub and popular tourist destination. There are various ways to exchange currency in London, including through banks, exchange bureaus, and ATMs.

When it comes to using foreign ATMs in London, it's important to be aware of potential fees and criminal activity. Here are some tips to keep in mind:

- Use ATMs at banks or reputable financial institutions: Stick to ATMs located at banks or reputable financial institutions, as these are likely to have higher security measures in place to prevent criminal activity.
- Avoid standalone ATMs: Be cautious of standalone ATMs located on the street, as these are more susceptible to skimming and other forms of fraud.
- Use ATMs inside well-lit areas: Choose ATMs located inside well-lit areas, such as inside a bank

branch or shopping center, as these are less likely to be targeted by criminals.
- Use ATMs during daylight hours: Try to use ATMs during daylight hours when there are more people around, as this can deter potential criminals from targeting you.
- Look out for hidden fees: Be aware that some foreign ATMs may charge fees for withdrawals, so make sure to read the terms and conditions carefully before using them. It's also a good idea to check with your bank beforehand to see if they have any partnerships with forcign banks that offer fee-free withdrawals.

Overall, it's important to exercise caution when using foreign ATMs in London to avoid excessive fees and criminal activity. By following these tips and being aware of your surroundings, you can help ensure a safe and smooth currency exchange experience.

Printed in Great Britain
by Amazon